WORLD OF
REPTILES

IGUANAS

by **Sophie Lockwood**

Content Adviser: Harold K. Voris, PhD, Curator and Head,
Amphibians and Reptiles, Department of Zoology,
The Field Museum, Chicago, Illinois

THE CHILD'S WORLD®, CHANHASSEN, MINNESOTA

IGUANAS

Published in the United States of America by The Child's World®
PO Box 326 • Chanhassen, MN 55317-0326 • 800-599-READ • www.childsworld.com

Acknowledgements:

The Child's World®: Mary Berendes, Publishing Director

Editorial Directions, Inc.: E. Russell Primm, Editorial Director; Pam Rosenberg, Editor;
Judith Shiffer, Assistant Editor; Caroline Wood and Rory Mabin, Editorial Assistants;
Susan Hindman, Copy Editor; Emily Dolbear and Sarah E. De Capua, Proofreaders;
Elizabeth Nellums, Olivia Nellums, and Daisy Porter, Fact Checkers; Tim Griffin/
IndexServ, Indexer; Cian Loughlin O'Day, Photo Researcher, Linda S. Koutris, Photo
Editor

The Design Lab: Kathleen Petelinsek, Art Director and Cartographer; Julia Goozen, Page
Production Artist

Photos:

Cover: Corbis; frontispiece / 4: Ryan McVay / Stone / Getty Images.

Interior: Alamy Images: 5-top right and 17 (Dynamics Graphics Group / Creatas),
5-bottom right and 28 (M. Timothy O'Keefe), 5-bottom left and 37 (Stephen Frink
Collection), 11 (Wolfgang Pölzer), 33 (Atmotu Images); Animals Animals / Earth
Scenes: 15 (Peter Weimann), 18 (Studio Carlo Dani), 22 (Lynn D. Odell); Corbis: 2-3,
5-middle and 24 (Joe McDonald), 13 (Herbert Kehrer / zefa), 21 (Clive Druett / Papilio),
27 (Bettmann), 31 (Macduff Everton), 34 (David A. Northcott); Jeremy Woodhouse /
Photodisc / Getty Images: 5-top left and 8.

Library of Congress Cataloging-in-Publication Data

Lockwood, Sophie.
  Iguanas / by Sophie Lockwood.
    p. cm. — (The world of reptiles)
  Includes bibliographical references (p.   ) and index.
  ISBN 1-59296-548-2 (library bound : alk. paper)
  1. Iguanas—Juvenile literature. I. Title.
  QL666.L25L63 2006
  597.95'42—dc22   2005024790

TABLE OF CONTENTS

Chapter One

On the Galápagos Islands

Six hundred miles (966 kilometers) west of Ecuador, a line of islands emerges from the waves. The Galápagos Islands consist of thirteen major and six minor islands, and forty tiny clumps of land—islets—sticking out of the Pacific Ocean. This is a strange, eerie place. Mists cover volcanic craters and black sand beaches. Waves pound against cinder slopes and lava tunnels.

On the islands, creatures that exist nowhere else on Earth slither, creep, and flutter. A giant Galápagos tortoise munches prickly pear cactus. Flightless cormorants plunge into the Pacific in search of eels, fish, and octopus. Galápagos penguins—the only penguin species that lives on the equator—waddle to the shoreline. The islands have their own species of cotton, pepper, passionflower, and tomato plants. Daisies grow on trees. Hawks and barn owls swoop during the night, looking for rats, mice, and small lizards.

Marine Iguana Fast Facts
(Amblyrhynchus cristatus)
Adult length:
   Female: about 20 inches (60 cm)
   Male: 30 to 60 inches
      (75 to 150 cm)
Coloration: Gray-black with red,
   brown, and yellow splotches
Range: Galápagos Islands
Reproduction: 1 to 6 eggs per
   clutch
Diet: Seaweed

This map shows the habitats of select iguana species in the Americas.

Also at night, dark-skinned marine iguanas pile on top of each other on the rocky slopes leading down to the water. They are the only seagoing iguanas in the world and they are trying to stay warm.

As the sun rises, gray-black marine iguanas move around to find a spot in direct sunlight. They are reptiles—cold-blooded creatures. Iguanas cannot control their own body temperatures. They need sun to get warm. The large adult males slowly head down to the water. Some crawl over the rocks into the waves. Others crawl across the beaches and challenge the crashing surf.

Although the Galápagos lie along the equator, the water is cold. Deep underwater currents that started near Antarctica rise to the ocean's surface near the islands. The water is full of **nutrients** that make sea plants grow six times as fast here as in other areas. The Galápagos marine iguana population numbers between 200,000 and 300,000 and that means plenty of seaweed nibbling. Seaweed needs to grow quickly to feed so many hungry lizards.

By midmorning, adult males head for deep waters, about 300 feet (100 meters) offshore. Male marine iguanas grow to about 5 feet (1.5 m) long and are strong swimmers. Adult males dive up to 60 feet (20 m) deep to **forage** for seaweed. They can stay underwater up

The waters that surround the Galápagos Islands are cold, and marine iguanas spend a lot of time warming themselves in the sun after swimming.

to fifteen minutes. Female and **juvenile** iguanas graze on seaweed closer to shore and in tide pools. The water there is shallower but still cold. The iguanas don't stay in the water very long. The cold water lowers an iguanas' body temperature to dangerous levels. If an iguana gets too cold, it becomes sluggish. Then it will not be able to fight the surf to get back to shore.

By afternoon, the marine iguanas fight their way up the rocky cliffs to find a place in the warm sun. Dark volcanic stone holds the sun's warmth. Marine iguanas crawl over each other to find a patch of open rock.

Despite the harsh living conditions on the Galápagos Islands, marine iguanas thrive. **Predators** control the population. They attack marine iguana eggs and juveniles. Hawks, owls, mockingbirds, crabs, gulls, rats, and snakes feed on the young. Once marine iguanas reach adult size, however, they usually live long lives. Their expected life span is almost as long as a human's: sixty years or more.

One reason marine iguanas live so long is that they have a unique **metabolism.** When food is scarce on the Galápagos, marine iguanas stop growing. In fact, they start shrinking. Their

Did You Know?
After a morning of diving into the salt water to feed, marine iguanas have excess salt in their bodies. They have a special gland in their noses to take care of this—they sneeze away the extra salt.

bodies feed on their own muscles, fat, and bones. Marine iguanas switch from growth mode to shrink mode many times during their lives. The growing and shrinking of marine iguanas is just one more bizarre characteristic of the unusual Galápagos.

Marine iguanas usually dive underwater for five or ten minutes at a time when they feed.

Chapter Two

Green Dragons

Iguanas are lizards, reptiles, and members of the order Squamata. There are 650 to 700 species of iguanas in fifty-five different groups, or genera. Iguanids include regular iguanas, anoles, basilisks, sand and horned lizards, and ctenosaurs (spiny-tailed lizards). Iguanas live in many different habitats—in tropical rain forests, Caribbean paradises, sweltering deserts, and on bleak volcanic islands. Depending on the environment, iguanas vary in size, shape, appearance, feeding habits, and sleeping choices. They may live in burrows or trees or under rocks. Yet they all belong to the vast family of lizards called Iguanidae.

An iguana's length is measured from the head to the end of the tail. The tail is up to three times the length of the body. The animals often referred to as Madagascar iguanas are miniature versions of common green iguanas. They grow to about 7.5 inches (25 centimeters) long. On the Pacific island of Fiji, crested iguanas are about three times that size, measuring about 24 inches (75 cm) long.

Large iguanas include marine iguanas, which are about 5 feet (1.5 m) long, and green iguanas, which can be up to 7 feet (2.1 m) long.

When you think about iguanas, you probably think green. Most iguanas are shades of green, but there are also brown, gray, and blue iguanas. An iguana's color doesn't just come from the surface. Green hues come from yellow and blue **pigments** in iguana skin. The color iguanas present is like mixing paint. More yellow and less blue makes for a pale green. Green males tend to have duller colors than females. The most vivid color of all appears

Madagascar iguanas are small versions of the common green iguana.

on newborns. **Hatchlings** often emerge from their eggs a brilliant blue. As yellow pigment becomes more active, the newborns' colors turn to bright green.

Even green iguanas are not always green. Those that live in Central America have gray heads. Columbian iguanas have white heads, while a small group of South American iguanas are red-headed.

Desert iguanas tend to be tan, brown, and reddish-brown to blend with the desert sands and stones. Marine iguanas have brown, gray, or black skin with red markings. Rock iguanas are generally browns and grays to match the stones and soil where they live.

Like chameleons, iguanas change color with the temperature and their moods. In cool weather, iguanas turn darker because dark colors absorb more heat. In bright, hot sun, iguana skin becomes lighter because light colors reflect sun. Stress and anger also affect an iguana's color. A stressed-out iguana turns dark gray, dark brown, or black. These are not normal iguana shades. Color changes begin at the head and tail and move to the center.

Crawling and climbing are important for iguanas. Many species live in trees, and there is no way to get home

Green Iguana Fast Facts
(Iguana iguana)
Adult length: Up to 7.5 feet (2.1 m)
Coloration: Green with brownish-black bands
Range: Central and South America, some Caribbean islands
Reproduction: 25 to 60 eggs per clutch
Diet: Leaves, berries, fruits, and other plant material

Some Central American green iguanas have gray heads.

without climbing. Iguana legs are strong and muscular. Each foot has five toes with sharp talons. The claws help the iguana grasp tree bark as it climbs. Although iguanas don't have webbed toes, they are excellent swimmers.

Green and marine iguanas show a definite resemblance to dragons. Iguanas have blunt noses, somewhat flat heads, and teeth like saw blades. Most iguanas have crests on their backs and a row of ridges along the spine. When a male iguana feels threatened, the ridges rise. Few creatures look more like fierce dragons than threatened iguanas.

Like all reptiles, temperature changes can be a problem for iguanas. A cold reptile is slow and sluggish. A warm reptile is quick and agile. When predators lurk behind every bush, a speedy escape is important. So iguanas rely on the sun to help them maintain the right body temperature.

Lying in the sun is called basking. The average iguana basks most often in the afternoons. In the desert, however, iguanas sun in the morning, then hide in bushes to avoid scorching afternoon heat. At night, iguanas must find warm

Iguanas have long toes and sharp claws that help them climb up trees.

spots for sleeping. Piling on top of one another is one way to stay warm. Crawling under a warm stone or into a burrow is another.

Chapter Three

A Lizard's Life

In the Dominican Republic, a **clutch** of iguana eggs rested at the end of a 3-foot-long (90-cm-long) dirt tunnel. The twenty eggs incubated for about six months. All eggs in a clutch hatch at roughly the same time, so when it is time, 7-inch-long (17.5-cm-long) rhinoceros iguanas emerge.

The newborns are ready for action. That's a good thing, because their mother is not around to help. Once she laid her eggs and covered the nest with soil, she'd done her part. Hatchlings are on their own to find food, water, and safety.

The young rhino iguanas eat a more varied diet than their adult relatives. Hatchlings will eat insects, caterpillars, and other small creatures. They will also munch on leaves, flowers, and fruit. They get water from the plants they eat or by drinking rainwater out of puddles. Finding food is an immediate concern but not the biggest problem facing rhino iguana hatchlings.

Rhino iguanas dig their nests in the ground. But the Dominican Republic is a Caribbean resort island. Hotels, restaurants, and other resort facilities take over

Two rhino iguana hatchlings emerge from their eggs.

natural iguana habitats. So it is getting harder for iguanas to find places to bury their eggs. Hatchlings also face a variety of introduced predators. Dogs, cats, and pet birds prey on hatchlings. Humans do, too. They catch the babies to sell as pets.

Catching a hatchling isn't that hard. Rhino iguanas are **diurnal**—active during the day. While they browse among the plants, they can be seen and captured.

Catching young iguanas to sell as pets is against the law, but catching the poachers who collect iguanas is difficult. Many people on the island are poor. They can earn a year's salary in just a few weeks by collecting rhino iguana hatchlings. The money puts food on their tables and clothes on their children. For many, the risk of being arrested is worth it.

The journey from hatchling to adult takes several years. Most rhino iguanas are full grown when they reach 2 to 4 feet (60 to 120 cm) long. Because they are land dwellers, these iguanas are splotchy gray and brown. They have hornlike nubs on their noses and crests on the back of their heads. As adults, they prefer feeding on thorny plants, fruit, flowers, and cactus. In a pinch, they'll also eat insects and eggs.

Rhinoceros Iguana Fast Facts
(Cyclura cornuta cornuta)
Adult length: 24 to 48 inches (60 to 120 cm)
Coloration: Brown with thin, darker brown bands
Range: Haiti and the Dominican Republic (island of Hispaniola)
Reproduction: 5 to 20 eggs per clutch
Diet: Leaves, vegetation, flowers, fruit, eggs, and insects

By the time a female reaches five years old, she is ready to mate. Mating usually occurs in April. The soon-to-be mother finds a suitable male to fertilize her eggs. She then builds a nest similar to the tunnel-like home she normally lives in. She digs a 3-foot-long (90-cm-long) tunnel with a nesting room at the end. She'll lay from five to twenty eggs in the nest. Younger, smaller females lay fewer eggs than older, larger females.

DIFFERENT HABITATS, DIFFERENT LIVES

Rhinoceros iguanas live in lush tropical habitats. It rains regularly, so water is easily found. Plant growth seems to

Rhino iguanas get their name from the hornlike growths found on their heads.

A land iguana in the Galápagos Islands eats part of a cactus plant.

explode overnight, and food is plentiful. Other iguana species live in different habitats. Their lives present different demands.

The Galápagos Islands have two types of iguanas: marine and land. Land iguanas never venture into the sea for food. They live inland, away from the coastline. Some visitors have compared the Galápagos landscape to the moon's surface, so how do the land iguanas survive? They have to compete with other **herbivores** for cactus, flowers, and fruit. In years when food is scarce, some land iguanas starve.

A male land iguana stakes out a specific territory and challenges other males that try to take over his space. The owner bobs his head, bites the intruder, and uses his tail to whip the other male. Once his territory is secure, the male goes about mating with every female in his area.

A female digs a shallow nest and deposits two to twenty eggs. The chance of an egg becoming an adult is slim. Hawks, egrets, herons, and snakes eat eggs and hatchlings. At one point, the land iguana population was nearly wiped out by wild dogs.

Shelter is hard won. To escape the heat of the day, land iguanas lie in the shade of rocks, trees, or cactus. At night, they settle into shallow burrows to retain

Galápagos Land Iguana Fast Facts

(Conolophus subcristatus)

Adult length: More than 39 inches (1 m)

Coloration: Brown back with yellow or orange legs and belly

Range: Galápagos Islands

Reproduction: 2 to 20 eggs per clutch

Diet: Mainly cactus, other plants, and fruit

as much body heat as possible. If they survive to adulthood, Galápagos land iguanas may live more than fifty years.

IN THE DESERT

Desert iguanas thrive in the desert regions of Nevada, California, and Arizona. They have rounder bodies than their tropical relatives. Desert iguanas are short—about 10 to 16 inches (25 to 40 cm) long—with whitish splotches on brownish skin. The tails are usually tan banded with dark brown.

Desert iguanas survive in a harsh land where water is scarce and even plants are not always available. They live among sand, rocks, and creosote bushes. When the sun scorches the desert, the iguanas crawl up into bushes where it is a bit cooler. Desert nights bring low temperatures. The iguanas often take over rodent burrows at night. The warm earth protects the iguanas from extreme cold.

Food and water are obvious problems for desert dwellers. The desert iguana has adapted by eating foods other iguanas wouldn't touch. Cactus, thorny bushes, grasses, fruits, and flowers make up their main meals.

They also eat insects, beetles, and dead animals. Even rotting flesh has protein, minerals, and water needed for survival.

Desert iguanas can tolerate higher temperatures than most other desert reptiles.

Chapter Four

When Columbus Arrived

Columbus made his remarkable voyage to what he believed to be a New World in 1492. Up to that point, Europeans had no knowledge of iguanas. When the Spaniards first arrived, the native people of the West Indies—the Taino—raised iguanas as meals for nobles. The Spanish took one look and decided that iguanas were too ugly to eat.

Not so, said the Taino. Barbecued iguana was a gourmet treat. Eventually, the Taino convinced the Spanish to try roasted iguana, and many Spaniards liked it. In 1526, Gonzalo de Oviedo wrote of his iguana experiences: "The animal is better to eat than to see," and the taste was "as good or better than rabbit."

The Taino believed iguanas played a role in the creation of their culture. Their **creation myth** claims that Macoel was the guardian of the cave from which the Tainos first emerged.

Christopher Columbus comes ashore on the island of San Salvador.

Macoel's name meant *"eyes that did not blink."* As a guard, he was excellent because he saw everything. Macoel was a reptile, and iguana. He sat completely still, his skin gray-brown and mottled like the cave's stone walls.

Visitors to Aruba's Arikok National Park can see this lizard drawing created by a Taino artist.

The lizard, Macoel, had a third, all-seeing eye. Yet, one night, Macoel ignored his duties. Instead of guarding the cave, he left his post. The next day, the sun turned Macoel to stone for failing in his job.

Rock iguanas that live in the West Indies have a scaly patch on their foreheads. That patch could well be the "all-seeing eye" of the Taino legend. One thing is certain. The word *iguana* comes to us from the Taino word *higuana*. *Gua* referred to nobles, gods, and golden ones. For the Taino, the iguana was a noble, golden animal that later served as a major food source for the island people. They honored higuana by drawing its picture on cave walls.

Cultures that admired iguanas recognized the lizard's patience and understanding. Clans that chose the iguana as their totems, or symbols, did so because life in their native lands required great patience and understanding. Not every day was a successful hunting day. Not every crop produced a great harvest. Life required patience. Perhaps that is why the Maya represented Itzam Na, one of their major gods, as an iguana or lizard. A true god also needed patience in guiding his people.

Chapter Five

Man and Iguanas

By the 1970s, scientists believed that the Jamaican rock iguana was **extinct**. None had been seen for more than thirty years. Then in 1970 and again in 1990, living specimens were sighted in the remote Hellshire Hills section of Jamaica, a limestone forest wilderness. Scientists took a census and counted about 100 lizards.

One hundred animals is a small population for an entire species. Small numbers create a very small gene pool. This means that breeding males end up mating with their own daughters. Over several generations, mating with close relatives could lead to physical problems carried in genes.

Zoos and **conservation** groups quickly developed a recovery and captive breeding program. Scientists make sure that males mate with as many different females as possible. In the wild, this would be impossible, as dominant males would mate often and weaker males would never mate at all. It is hoped that careful breeding will develop a stronger, healthier species.

Jamaican Rock Iguana Fast Facts

(Cyclura collei)

Adult length: Up to 36 inches (90 cm)

Coloration: Light or reddish brown with blue or green highlights

Range: Jamaica

Reproduction: 16 to 20 eggs per clutch

Diet: Leaves, fruits, flowers, and, occasionally, snails

The Grand Cayman blue iguana is in great danger of becoming extinct.

Hatchlings live in safe breeding pens until they are old enough to survive in the wild. They must learn to hunt for themselves, dig burrows, and avoid predators. For iguanas, these skills come from **instinct.** They do not learn hunting or digging from their mothers. If the protective environment in which the Jamaican iguana hatchlings live is enough like their natural habitat, the babies should easily return to nature.

THREATS TO SURVIVAL

Different iguana species range from being plentiful in the wild (the common green iguana) to critically endangered (Ricord's iguana and Anegada iguana). Most rock iguana species are endangered in the wild. Threats to survival come from a range of sources, including humans, cattle, and even goats.

The Fiji crested iguana and the Anegada iguana have lost livable habitat due to goats. Humans brought goats to Fiji and the British Virgin Islands as farm animals. They graze on anything, and they are extremely sure-footed, even on rocky cliffs. It would seem that goats would be ideal. Unfortunately, goats eat the same food as iguanas, only more of it. They can clear an area quicker than a tractor.

Resorts on Caribbean islands also take away habitat. Puerto Rican iguanas and Navassa Island iguanas are two species that are now extinct due to building and other human activities.

The Fiji crested iguana is losing habitat to goats that were brought to the island as farm animals.

Spiny-tailed iguanas are often bad-tempered.

In some cases, humans have brought pets into iguana territories. Dogs, cats, and pet birds present serious threats to iguanas. Some pets roam wild. They kill iguanas for food. In Jamaica, mongooses were brought in for snake control, but they also kill iguanas.

The most damaging predators are humans. Humans collect iguanas of all species for pets. While it is true that most reptile pets are captive bred, many are also captured in the wild. Iguanas usually make good pets, but some species never adjust to pet life. Spiny-tailed iguanas, for example, are bad-tempered and can be vicious. The best place for wild animals is in the wild. It is where they belong.

HOPE FOR THE FUTURE

Iguanas may yet outlive the trials of survival. Critically endangered and endangered species have recovery programs. These programs provide a breeding and survival plan for animals in the wild. The plans set up new iguana populations in national parks or nature preserves. Zoos take part in breeding programs in which they trade adult males to breed stronger genetic profiles in the overall species population.

Eggs of endangered species are collected in the wild. Those eggs are incubated in nurseries. The hatchlings are raised in safe surroundings. Instead of losing 80 to 90 percent of eggs and hatchlings to predators, scientists are able to raise 90 percent to adulthood.

The Center for International Trades in Endangered Species (CITES) lists many iguana species as endangered or threatened. In some cases, such as green iguanas, CITES recommends that countries limit the number of animals exported for pet trade. Those iguanas that are exported should be from licensed reptile breeders, not captured in the wild. For most rock iguana species, CITES prohibits capture and sale of the animals or their body parts.

What is your role in saving iguanas? You can support conservation groups, such as Defenders of Wildlife or the World Wildlife Federation. If you visit a known iguana habitat, do not try to catch or disturb an iguana. Finally, if you think having an iguana would be great, learn all

A girl carefully observes marine iguanas in their natural habitat.

you can about iguanas before getting one. Then, only buy from a licensed breeder so that you know your iguana was bred to be a pet, not stolen from the wild.

Glossary

clutch (KLUHCH) a group of eggs laid at one time

conservation (kon-sur-VAY-shuhn) the act of saving or preserving some aspect of wildlife

creation myth (kree-AY-shuhn MITH) a story about how the world began

diurnal (dye-UR-nuhl) active in the daytime

extinct (ek-STINGKT) a plant or animal that no longer exists

forage (FOR-ij) to search for food

hatchlings (HACH-lingz) newborns that emerge from eggs

herbivores (HUR-buh-vorz) plant eaters

instinct (IN-stingkt) one's natural sense of what is happening with one's body, or actions one takes

juvenile (JOO-vuh-nuhl) a youngster, like a human toddler

metabolism (muh-TAB-uh-liz-uhm) the bodily process of turning food into energy

nutrients (NOO-tree-uhnts) the value in food that is used by the body

pigments (PIG-muhnts) substances that create a color or hue

predators (PRED-uh-turz) animals that hunt and kill other animals for food

For More Information

Watch It

Green Iguanas. VHS (Hauppauge, N.Y., Barron's Educational, 1999).

World's Last Great Places: Galapagos Islands, Land of Dragons. VHS (Washington, D.C., National Geographic).

Read It

Barter, James. *The Galápagos Islands*. San Diego: Lucent Books, 2002.

Claybourne, Anna. *Lizards*. Chicago: Raintree, 2004.

Louise, Sara. *Giant Lizards*. Logan, Iowa: Perfection Learning, 2001.

Look It Up

Visit our home page for lots of links about iguanas:
http://www.childsworld.com/links

Note to Parents, Teachers, and Librarians: We routinely verify our Web links to make sure they are safe, active sites—so encourage your readers to check them out!

The Animal Kingdom
Where Do Iguanas Fit In?

Kingdom: Animal

Phylum: Chordata

Class: Reptilia

Order: Primates

Family: Squamata

Genus: *Iguanidae*

Species: There are hundreds of iguana species

Index

About the Author

Sophie Lockwood is a former teacher and a longtime writer. She writes textbooks, newspaper articles, and magazine articles. Sophie enjoys writing about animals and their habits. The most interesting part of her research, Sophie says, is learning how scientists apply their knowledge to save endangered species. She lives with her husband in the foothills of the Blue Ridge Mountains.